THE POWER OF CHOICE

DR. J.L. WILLIAMS

Copyright © 2014 by Dr. J.L. Williams

The Power of Choice
by Dr. J.L. Williams

Printed in the United States of America

ISBN 9781498400046

All rights reserved solely by the author. The author guarantees all contents are original and do not infringe upon the legal rights of any other person or work. No part of this book may be reproduced in any form without the permission of the author. The views expressed in this book are not necessarily those of the publisher.

Scripture.quotations taken from the King James Version of the Bible. Scripture marked NKJV is taken from the New King James Version. Copyright 1982 by Thomas Nelson, Inc. Used by permission. All rights reserved.

www.xulonpress.com

PREFACE

THIS IS PART ONE OF A FOUR-PART SERIES ENTITLED
THE POWER SERIES.

DEDICATION

Do you want wholeness in your life? Do you want to change the course of your life? Do you think it's just not possible to be happy or successful, or to have a more meaningful relationship in your life? You can, because you have "The Power of Choice."

TABLE OF CONTENTS

Personal 15
Financial 17
Education 19
Spiritual 21

Power: The ability or capacity to act or perform effectively.
Choice: The power, right, or liberty of choosing.

On an average day, have you ever thought about how many choices are made by the average individual? Multiply that number by 365 days a year, and the power of choice will be an astounding number!

To choose or not to choose is still a choice, because whether you choose to do something or you choose not to do something, either way, you have made a choice!

Choices—they are something that we do countless times a day. Some choices may seem more significant than others, but nevertheless, they are choices.

The Power of Choice

(PERSONAL)

Definition of the word personal: Relating to, or affecting a person, relating to an individual or his character, conduct.

Choices that are made, although personal, will affect others that you associate with either directly or indirectly. Personal also deals with one's conduct, and although it is "personal" it will still directly or indirectly affect other people (family, friends, coworkers, etc.) Some personal choices that we make can be totally selfish.

We are not concerned about how others will be affected. Example: A young woman goes off with a young man that may not be the right individual for her. As the young woman, you may feel that it is your personal choice with whom you get involved with. Friends and parents may try to give you advice or sound warnings about this personal choice you have made, but being a totally selfish individual by your personal choice, it may cause a lot of dismay and concerns on your parents' and friends' part. If you are a person who believes that it is your way or the highway, and will not accept advice or warnings from friends and parents, well...you may regret your choice down the road.

Remember the saying; "No man is an island." One does not succeed or fail in life by one's self. Other people contribute to your success or your failure in life. Who do you associate with? What kinds of individuals do you spend the majority of your time with? The people that you associate with, and spend the majority of your time with, can sometimes influence the personal choices that you make in life.

You choose your own destiny; your choices will define who you will become.

The Power of Choice

(FINANCIAL)

This is an area where a lot of us struggle. Handling your finances in a proper, responsible way can and will reap great rewards. When I am talking finances, I am talking about simply, money. Money is simply a resource or currency that is used to purchase goods and services. And in our society, it is something vital to our survival. Therefore, you have the power of choice on how you handle it. Money can be both a blessing, and a curse. It is a blessing when it is properly handled, and it is a curse when it is not properly handled. At the base of human survival, according to theory, we as humans need shelter, food, and clothing to survive in the world. We need to have a roof over our heads, food to eat, and clothes to wear. We also have responsibilities for ourselves and family. Therefore, unless you have been born with the proverbial "silver spoon," you and I have to find honest, gainful employment to create enough finances to sustain survival in this world. The power of choice is yours as to how you are going to achieve financial stability. You must be disciplined and make wise investments. Example: choices from buying a loaf of bread, to buying a car or a house.

The Power of Choice

(EDUCATIONAL)

Have you ever heard the saying, "A mind is a terrible thing to waste"? Well, it is a true saying. When you choose not to get a good quality education, you are wasting your mind. The definition of education is: The action or process of educating or being educated.

Another definition is: The knowledge and development resulting from an educational process. Our brain is like a computer. It can store lots of information. Each of us has the power as to what kind of information we store in our brain. You and I have the power of choice. Education is something that no one can ever take away from you. It is something that is very valuable to have in today's world.

Without education, it would be very hard to survive. You would be a target for others to take advantage of you. For example, if you don't know how to do simple math, you are a target for crooked businessmen, con artists, and the like. If you cannot do simple math, (addition, subtraction, multiplication, and division) you will be like a mortally wounded animal watching the crooked businessmen and con artists, who would be the vultures circling around you ready to attack and finish you off.

You are at a severe disadvantage if you do not know how to read and write. In today's world, you must equip yourself with the proper tools (quality education) to survive and compete in our world. Technology is getting faster and faster and of a higher quality.

Therefore, you should want to give yourself a fighting chance. However, you and only you can make the decision to receive a quality education. You have the power of choice. The more education you have, the more valuable you become.

The Power of Choice

(SPIRITUAL)

Spiritual: Things that pertain to a spiritual, ecclesiastical, or religious nature.

Spiritual choices: Making the right choice concerning your spiritual and eternal destination.

Man is a threefold being: Man is a spirit, has a soul, and lives in a body (physical house). Man was created for a purpose, and that purpose was to serve God. You are created in God's image and likeness, created in the image of God-like-ness (Godliness). After righteousness (Genesis 1:26-31). Once we find out who we really are, we will know that we are more than conquerors. Truth defines us. You and I are defined by the truth.

What is truth? God's Word is truth. Jesus said, "I am the way, the truth, and the life" (St. John 14:6). We have an image problem. The enemy (Satan) has distorted our perception as to who we are. He is making us to believe that we are worthless, no-good, conquered individuals. The enemy does not want you to look in God's mirror of who you really are, but he wants you to look in his mirror, which is very distorted.

The Power of Choice

Some choices you cannot change:
1. Your race

2. What family you are born into
3. Your ancestry.

Choices that you CAN change:

1. Your behavior
2. Your contribution to society
3. Not choosing to be a success.

Examples of poor excuses used by some individuals for their choice of not being successful:
1. I was born on the wrong side of the tracks
2. I am of a minority race
3. I'm just not good enough

Don't be a negative statistic, but strive to be a positive one.

Don't allow the negative labels society places on you discourage you. Prove the labels wrong!

The choices that we make will carry enormous consequences.

Should I be a law-abiding citizen? Or a lawbreaker?

Should I have premarital sex, or wait until I am married?

Should I get involved in drugs and alcohol, or stay and maintain a healthy, drug-free lifestyle?

Should I continue my education, or should I drop out?

Should I waste my life, or make my life productive and successful?

Should I just party my life away, or should I have a more disciplined lifestyle?

Should I be texting and talking on a cell phone while driving, or put my full attention on my driving?

Should I go out to dinner, or should I have dinner at home?

Should I help others, or hurt them?

Should I speak well of someone, or speak ill of someone?

Should I be critical or judgmental of someone, or not?

Should I forgive, or not?

Should I leave a positive mark on society, or a negative one?

Should I be a mentor for others, or not?

Should I be an inspiration to others in a positive way, or a negative one?

Should I be a hard worker with a good attitude, or a lazy worker with a negative attitude?

How many red lights in life are you going to run before something happens?

Should I choose to make wise investments or not?

Should I choose to plan my life, or live life spontaneously (Or by the seat of your pants)?

The power of choice: People have made countless decisions that affect the course of history.

Columbus deciding to sail west from Europe to find a sea route to the eastern hemisphere, and then bumping into the western hemisphere instead. The world hasn't been the same since Europeans colonized North America.

The coin toss, it's a 50/50 chance, heads or tails. This ritual is done before football games to see which team will receive the opening kickoff.

J. P. Richardson, also known as "The Big Bopper," won a coin toss in February 1959 to secure a seat in the ill-fated flight of Buddy Holly. Richie Valens won the coin toss to Buddy Holly's guitarist (Waylon Jennings). The plane, taking off in a blinding snowstorm, crashed into a cornfield, instantly killing Holly, Richardson, Valens, and the twenty-one-year-old pilot.

You have the power of choice in the following areas:

- Political parties that you belong to
- Humanitarian organizations that you support
- Charitable organizations that you contribute to
- Public education or private?
- Hobbies?
- Sports?
- Free time?
- What kind of neighborhood do you wish to live in? Busy neighborhood, quiet neighborhood, or gated neighborhood?

The Power of Choice:

(WHAT STREET DO YOU LIVE ON?)

Arrogant Avenue
Blessing Blvd.
Carefree Circle
Destiny Drive
Happiness Highway
Hardship Heights
Handout Highway
Lazy Lane
Pathetic Place
Rejection Road
Regret Route
Success Street
Sleepy Street
Triumphant Terrace
Whatever Way

The location or street that you live on in life results from the choice you have made—the power of choice.

You have the power; it lies within you. You have "The Power of Choice!"

AUTHOR'S BIOGRAPHY

Dr. J. L. Williams is an associate minister at the New Zion M. B. Church of Clearwater, Florida. He is the author of Messages of Inspiration Volumes I and II, which currently have been translated into eleven different languages and are also in three foreign countries.